BEIR BUA 2021 Press

Fanny B. Mine

by

Best wishes,

Nikki Dudley

Published by Beir Bua Press

Dedication

for all the strong women I know

ISBN: 978-1-914972-18-8

Beir Bua Press, Co. Tipperary, Ireland.

Typesetting / Layout, Cover design: Michelle Moloney King

Cover image - Michelle Moloney King

Ordering Information: For details, see www.BeirBuaPress.com

Published by Beir Bua Press

Printed in the UK
Our printer is certified as a B Corporation to measure our impact on the environment and help drive us to be even more conscious of our footprint.

9 781914 972188

Keats

My secondary school was right beside Hampstead Heath in North London. When my English teacher started teaching us about Keats, I would stare out the window and imagine him wandering around the Heath writing poems. It made me feel reassured by who I wanted to be - a poet, a thinker, someone who loved words. It made me feel more normal in this state school in the middle of London, where in sixth form, people would laugh at me in English when I answered questions!

I found a lot of comfort in Keat's words, especially his neuroses and his fears, the fact that he wasn't sure about his own abilities, as well as his love for nature and his talent for turning ideas on their heads with his uncertainty. What also struck me when reading his letters though was his jealousy concerning his love, Fanny Brawne. His lack of confidence sometimes made him mean in his letters. I sometimes wondered what would have happened if they had met in modern times - whether Fanny would have grown tired of the jealousy. What would have happened if Keats hadn't died so young? In a later letter, Fanny even mentions that perhaps she 'overrated' Keats in her younger life.

This collection is the result of these musings. Despite my huge respect for Keats, this collection is a series of reflections, responses, reimaginings and play in the context of Keats and Brawne having met in the modern day. It was so much fun to create and I really hope you'll enjoy the journey.

As you read this, please keep Keat's words about negative capability in mind, which he described as the capacity of being in: "uncertainties, mysteries, doubts, without any irritable reaching after fact and reason."

A Modern Love Story

@Fannyfabulous -

Will you be a fan-a-me?

>   (Sorry – sounded so
>   much better in my
>   head…)

I have 1289 followers on *Twitter*. I can improve UR algorithms OFC.

I will like all UR photos on Insta.

>   (I have 401 followers
>   on there).

I'll make *TikTok* videos dedicated 2 you. People will be like OMG LMAO but

>   I won't care.

You know, I read poems on *YouTube* too. Why don't you subscribe?

>   (SPOILER: some of
>   them are about U).

Let's link our socials, Fanny. Let's put 'in a relationship' on *Facebook*.

>   (Does anyone still
>   use it?)

Let's tag each other in photos and comments.

Let's get synced online. People will totally ship us but IRL.

Fanny, dear Fanny, are you signed up 2 *Tinder*?

We can delete our profiles together.
        Let's swipe right

                                        in person.

Pls @ me soon. My DMs are always open for U.

@Hopelessromantic / John

How we met

A ---- is full of ----------- / faces.

--- are a current in my --------, static.

Do I -------- you?

Butter wouldn't -----on your ------.

Love is a ----- I knew. ----- is new.

Cannot read a room full of expressions. Love is ▮▮▮▮▮▮▮▮▮▮▮▮▮▮▮▮▮▮▮▮▮▮▮
At that moment, the future is a rush of blood to the lungs.

A room full of faces, expressions couldn't read.

Words flowed, current buzzes.

Still. Your name fingertip static. Can I remember how you looked? Unconventional creases -

butter dripped under your stare.

T?he room faces / ?Expressions read /

?tatic of my fingers /   hum hum / T?hrough me /L?ove I knew /L

?ove is a word /

?urn me butter

Love a word. I knew.

knew?

The space empty of bodies. Blankness I can write. I am a stillness that settles over you.

Never. My face is moving on the tips of your toes.

Hate is a sentence you didn't know. Hate is sentence old.

Your avoidance is like lard would inflame.

MOUTH IS BAD & GOOD.

YOU
HAVE TOLERABLE FEET.

JUST THE BEGINNING

your first **breakthrough** MOMENTS

MANIPULATIVE FLOWERS MATTER

DEEPER, DARKER, LIKE NEVER BEFORE. *VOICE OF GENIUS*

IT ALL HAPPENED

AND FELL IN LOVE

BREAKS DOWN HOW
IT ENDS SMALL *unacknowledged man*

connected with **countdown** BLOOD

DO WE HAVE FREE WILL?

LOVE AMBITION AND POETRY

Love (synonyms: misery, unhappiness, treachery, apathy)

1: *(verb instrans)* Bend, bow, make an obeisance (to); stoop; *fig.* submit (to).

2: *(adjective)* Not highly, or not pretentiously, intellectual or cultured.

Ambition (synonyms: lethargy, aversion, idleness, humility)

1: *(noun)* Hesitation, doubt, uncertainty to one's course; an instance of double meaning; an expression having more than one meaning.

2: *(noun)* Impaired vision, without apparent change in the eye.

Poetry (synonyms: prose, prosaic speech/writing)

1: *(noun phr)* A poet who is insufficiently appreciated by his or her contemporaries.

2: (noun) The cultivation or growing of a beard.

I know not where to go

How do I love thee? Lemme me peel
                      your skin like a banana.
                            Count the ways
                    you're bruised.

I wanna feel the inside
when
the bulb swings back
#livingmybestlife / I see

                  the shutter snap snap snap

Did you use a filter? My eyes thought: perchance speak, kneel,
touch, kiss…

Is this Stockholm Syndrome?
To the woman
        who [captured] my attention
                with a to-wit-to-wooooooooo

> **I AM A SENTRY
> TO YOUR FORTRESS
> but are you
> really in
> there? Are you alive
> with filters?**

Do I drip with blood, blood
from a vampire's teeth
hiding in my mouth, hiding in
yours

        horseman / hawk / hound / awake.
though i carry your heart with me now
                  (i carry it in **my heart)**

Did we plan this? Moved the squares

and now can't remember where this began.

CHECK MATE.

Just know I love. You.

Shall I compare thee to a ripened plum? Nah, you're a
bibliography to every word. Every word wraps like heavy
roots. Rough winds do shake my darling
but we have credible references.

PLEASE NOTE: YOU ARE A FULLY DETONATED ROSE.
                          The fuckin colours, man.

                                              Am I afraid
                                    we'll grow old together?
                                                        Or
                                          that we won't?

Letter me with initials. Melt into me until the parts
are conjoined. An inoperable tumour.
A tumour that would die 4 love.

            How do I love thee? Let me
                    unpeel you,
                    undress you,
                    unadvertise you.

Scars call me

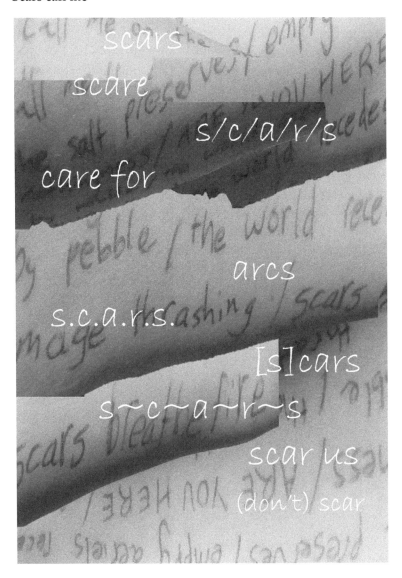

To Fanny.

I lament your mercy—pivot—lout!—ay, lout!
Merchandise love that tantalises nostalgia
one-thoughted, newcomer wandering, guillotine love,
unmanacled, and being see-through—without a bloomer!
O! lesser me have thee woof,—allay—allay—be mine!
That shan't, that fajita, that sweet minority zero
of lovesick, your Kirschner value ,—those hamsters, those
eyeless dividends,
that warning, whistling, lucid, million-pleasured breakfast,—
yourself—your souffle—in pity give me all,
wither no atom's ATM or I dielectric,
or living on, perfuse, your wretched throw,
forgo, in the mist of idiotic misdoubt,
life's purl,—the palaver of my mincemeat
losing its gut, and my ambiguity blinks!

The calendar of a dying man (part 1)

MONTHS MONTHS MONTHS

I am leading a post-human

               -humous

                   -haunted existence.

Doctor, give me a pen, not a scalpel. The colour of blood a death

warrant me a love to hold me – in fever dreams – if I must die if I must die, Fanny –

bind me to you in records

             we cannot ███████

The heart is bursting   aortal blood

                 haemorrhage you & me / on

               the edge of the page / a damn

                     sell breaks

YOU ARE MONSTROUSLY BEAUTIFUL

Your unrestrained

mouth. Don't put your lips near his ears

               (i tell you, his ears are

               a whisper of mine.)

next to of course chapman's homer fanny I love you woman
of unconventional beauty and so forth oh upon my soul
i can think of nothing else i cannot exist without you
now they're walking in parks and i can't think
then i felt like some watcher of the skies when a new planet
swims in love is my religion love is my religion my love
is selfish yet never did I breathe its pure serene till i heard
chapman speak, you fear, sometimes, I do not love you
so much as you wish? i cannot breathe without you and I
close my eyes when you look at him and silent upon a peak
fanny you are elegant, graceful, silly, fashionable and strange.

He wrote. And examined the blood spots on his pillow.

THE NEXT CHAPTER

A GUIDE TO SECOND DATE SEX

beam down, see who's there

SPOILERS!

FREE SPACE

Hands

Brains

delayed

reimagined

PARASITE

TALKING ABOUT TREES
into the mainstream

WARNING! Visceral but tender

reminding us to breathe'

HUNT *Enigma*

AND QUOTE
HEARTBREAKING *ignorance*

<u>Failed Haiku</u>

Oh Fanny, my dear,
Can I surmise you in brief?

…No. It appears not.

Fanny if by any other name

The relationship algorithm:

poor poet + fanny brawne = <u>DOES NOT COMPUTE!</u>

Listen though, no one puts Fanny in

      an equation

          in the corner of the world where I stand alone
and – YOU?

          ARE / MY /

            WORD

                    for
                everything.

…but but but

in American, your name is mud.

SIMILAR NAMES:

[Ahem] buttocks, nates, arse, butt, backside, bum, buns, can,
fundament, hindquarters, hind end, keister, posterior, prat,
rear, rear end, rump, stern, seat, tail, tail end, tooshie, tush,
bottom, behind, derriere, fanny, ass *(noun)*

They are backwards to your

beauty, chasing the tail of

bones seeping good.

They are bums to your good and bad mouth.

[I dream of your good bad mouth]

In hindsight, you will be no hindquarters.

They don't understand your fundamental fabulous fanny,
your post-era name, you have rear-ended me

ï ï ï ï ï ï ï ï ï ï ï ï ï ï ï

ï ï ï ï ï ï ï ï ï ï ï ï ï ï ï ï

My brain has hit the writing wall.

PLEASE SWITCH ME OFF AND ON AGAIN BECAUSE I
CAN'T STOP FALLING IN LOVE.

NAME INFO

Meaning: 'free one' in French.

You are a free one and I can't cannot will not shall never

pin you

to a deaf eh? Near shunned.

I change my mind about you as often as

I brush my teeth but do I really

do I really ever

spit you out? You swirl

    into my ink

        without a

    thought, like

        invisible ink

    that leaves

a stain.

    POPULARITY: Fanny is currently not ranked.

Judy could've given Fanny a chance but she thought the name
was bollocks. [Bitch.]

HONEY, HONEY, HONEY- Your name, your face, the slant of
your *F*

is love geometry[2]

but I can't

count the number of you

in algorithms and likes and thumbs up.

              (Do our profiles match on

                  Love Harmony?

*Sorry but... [*Shh*] - *"in England `fanny' is vulgar slang for female genitals."*

Then to really ruin the party...

ANTONYMS

Love pistol, penis, anaconda, baby's arm, bacon bazooka, bald-headed yogurt slinger, cock, joystick, lap rocket, limp bizkit, love gun, love muscle, love rod, lovestick

[Honestly, I don't even want to talk about this... Though maybe 'Love gun'...?]

Don't listen to the #haters, Fanny.

COMMENTS

Honestly I've always seen this as a bully's name. Something about it just reminds me of a big bad bully.

[They have never met you]

It sounds stuffy and nasally to me, and rather snobby as well.

[You wouldn't love me if you were stuffy and you do, don't you...?]

This is my mother's name. Although I won't be using it for any of my children, I think it is a classy name that is cute on a little girl, but seamlessly ages into an elegant and distinguished name for a woman. Except I hate Frankie and Fanny. Just kills the spunky yet pretty vibe the name gives.

[You are spunky, my love]

I really like this because it is unisex, but it's not.

[Um, yeah]

Anyway, shut up, world.

Your name is

my preposition, my conjunction, my un

>-doing. Intensify our relations before I

>get reflexive and fail

>to find the stem of

>me & you.

I'll rename myself

before I ever   rename you.

Throw me to the wind

bride of quietness,

silence slow time,

express

A tale sweetly

What haunts

mortals

What

mad struggle to escape?

What ecstasy?

Heard unheard

sensual ear

no tone:

beneath the trees

bare

Lover, never, never kiss,

grieve

fade,

love !

happy, happy

adieu;

For ever

warm and still

panting,

breathing passion

a heart

burning tongue.

█████████████████████ sacrifice?

████████████████ mysterious ████

████████████████████████ skies,

████████████████████████

What ██████████████ shore,

████████████████████

Is emptied ████████████████?

████████████ streets ████████

███ silent ███████████

Why ████████████████ return.

O ████ shape! ████████████

████████████████████

████ forest branches ████████████

████ silent form, ████ tease us ████ thought

████████████████

When ████████████████ waste,

████████████ in midst of ████ woe

████████████████████████████

"Beauty is truth, ██████████ that is all

████████████████

ANNOTATIONS ON A POET

✳ Can't hide truth!

Love won't stay
perfect

Fully - formed
plan?

HUMAN LINK

isolation with
these thoughts

Content
until she saw him

REALITY / DREAM?

CORRUPTED

lying in bed,
waiting

beauty dies!

incomplete / eerie /
deliberate

Almost as though
dying himself

Unhappy ending?

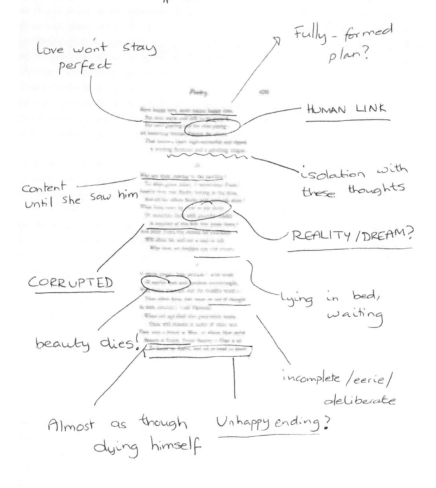

✳ when realise mortal,
realise really alone.

The calendar of a dying man (part 2)

WEEKS WEEKS WEEKS

1	2	3	4	5	6	7
Draw your features with words.	x	x	A calligram of you	x	x	the plague, pages and pages
8	**9**	**10**	**11**	**12**	**13**	**14**
x	between	the	spaces	x	I store [you] like acorns	… acorns lost in the soil
15	**16**	**17**	**18**	**19**	**20**	**21**
untold worth when the shroud	soaks up contami nated blood	x	from every pore	x	I cannot exist without U	Can U exist?
22	**23**	**24**	**25**	**26**	**27**	**28**
x	Arterial blood snatches you from me	and me from you and future from me	x	and what will be your future?	x	Oh fuck.
29	**30**					
The last page was torn	from my book					

Dear John,

Look, I'm really into you. You're so brooding and you use words I haven't heard before. (~~I spent twenty minutes after we last saw each other Googling words!~~) I enjoy spending time with you and yeah, I think we could really be something. <u>Maybe.</u> You know, I'm quite young but I like your letters, and videos, and texts, and DMs etc…

Maybe just lay off about the other guys. I've got to be able to go to parties without worrying you're going to be freaking out over my Insta pictures. ~~You're the one who keeps buggering off to the countryside to find yourself~~. I'll be here when you get back but in the meantime, I've got to be out with my friends.

I miss you too. Think about you loads. Remember the other day I sent you that thread about that actress and how she looked like different Pringle flavours? I knew you'd laugh at that.

Speak soon okay? And write soon.

Love, Fanny xxx

Fanny.

████████ Girl –

agreeable
eyes I
read your
assured
coldness: You
a little silent

Love
my pleasure and torment.
violent █ rush of blood
nearly suffocated – I
might not survive
thought
this is unfortunate

other subjects have entered my head

Your affectionate
J.K –

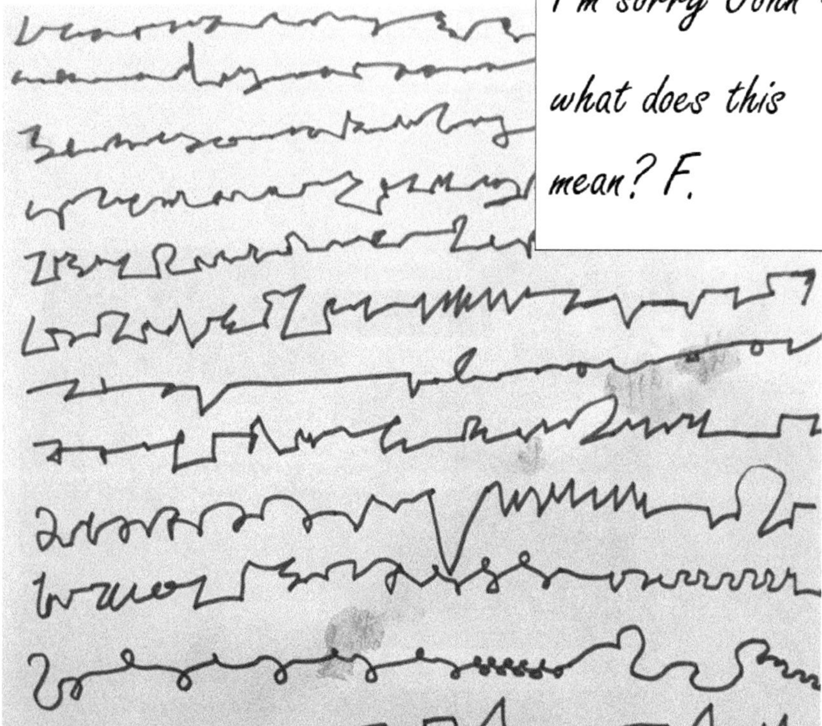

I'm sorry John –
what does this
mean? F.

Romantics Anonymous
online

Frank RA created group "Romantics Anonymous"

Frank RA added you

Frank

Everyone welcome John to the group!

Jac

Welcome John!

Becca

Hey John

Hari

Nice to meet ya

Rog

Nice to have new blood

Ula

Hey John. You single?

When I have fears that I may cease to be

Frank

Dude you're supposed to introduce yourself

Ula

I take that as a yes

Hari

Um, yeah. Bit heavy, man

Bright star! Would I were as steadfast

as thou art

Frank

Okay, John is a nice guy I promise. He just finds it hard to get out of his romantic mode

Becca

Got a lot of work to do, huh?

Awake for ever in a sweet unrest,

Still, still to hear her tender-taken breath

Frank

He's in love with a woman called Fanny

Rog

Fanny? Is that a real name?

Frank

Yeah, think so. They only met a few times

but he's super into her

Becca

A few times? Okay, perhaps a little fast, even

for us!

Frank

No judgement here

> Then on the shore of the wide world,
>
> I stand alone, and think till love and
>
> fame to nothingness do sink.

Hari

John, we're here for you.

Sounds like you need us.

Frank

Yep let's help him find his way guys

Beauty is truth, truth beauty

Becca

Seriously – does he ever stop doing that?

How are we meant to help him?

Frank

John – we'll start you on the steps

I have fears when

When I have fears that I... umm
Fears that I will... forget / you

>   Dear dear
>   Don't tell me.
>   Please.

When I have fears I fear:

- everything
- nothing
- all of the above

I am above you.

Fair creature, when I have fears   (Die, young
                                        bright star)

Is that the way to go? I have fears I shall
never   die young.

>   On the shore, I stand for
>   something.
Remember unreflecting, my love,
>   *are we done reflecting yet?*

When I have fears I fear nothing
Look upon you /// **LOOK AT ME**.

Cease cease
to be something / someone: remember my name when
     I HAVE FEARS.

Full ripe ungrained - I am unripened brain.
When I have pens on the shore *write you*.
                     Right, you loved me, yeah?

Teeming. I'm tearing inside. Before love and fame.
Nothing - in flames (us).

Look me up, creature. I am a creature but
                         is it fare?

Love:

- your face
- your fear.

                   My dear - I cease.

Des humains sans amour

—   a story has
no beginning &

no
e
n
d, ~~night at arms.~~
    where pain began
                    Alone & back to the point

  The sedge has withered   ███████████████
      the whisper

IN THE BRAIN,   Is it possible to fall in love
                                 over a dish of onions?

                    & no birds sing

The act of love itself has been described

        as the little death, *o what can ail thee!*

                            So haggard
                              & then
                    the door opened
                            & trust
                        came back.

*shh, love became 'onions'

& then the stair creaked,
& the harvest's done.

A police officer gathering evidence
         of a crime that hadn't yet been committed
                                  with anguish moist &
                                  fever dew.

Why doesn't hatred
kill desire? Full beautiful
– she had committed ~~nothing but~~
                         love.

hair was long, her foot was light & her head > sharply away.

Wished I had been able to whistle a tune, but
         // have no ear.

                                   Here, me, beautiful?

Set her under the cloth &
nothing saw
all day long.

                    For - unlike the rest -
              she was - unhaunted - by guilt.

She found me routes of remorse,
occupying no space,
&   sure   in   language strange   she
said –

*She looked as she did love.
& I wanted it to die quickly.*

            'H*pe y*u've g*t
             Everyth!ng
             y*u w@nt.'

She took me to her région étrange

(NOTE: I have no map)

& there she wept
   & sighed full sore,
   & there I couldn't bring down
   the curtain on the moment.
   & there she had no more capacity for love
   & there I wrote

     The latest dream I ever dreamt
      in a ditch out of view. I saw
  a jealous man, jealous even of the past, death-pale.

       I began to write.

No comment

   I saw starved lips in the affair,
with my (((eyes open)))
& I awoke &
    believed in sin,

          on the cold
            hill's
            side.

'Anyone who loves is jealous!'

     [& this is why there's no need ever to go back.]
   Alone & palely loitering
though the features
     blurred with
         our breath,

longing at the bright   & such

        unobtainable objects.

     !Leave me alone forever!

Fanny,

My sweet love, I shall wait patiently till tomorrow

assure you

time written

upon my mind

do I love you   In my
present state   separated
speak to you in

torment since I have known you

that suspicion
the surety of your Love,

Send me the words   my
pillow.

On Hampstead Heath, no one can hear you scream

Did I see love

        walking down the stairs?

            Did I see my love walking

            with a man last week under the trees

                on Hampstead Heath?

And when I saw love walking

        with a man on Hampstead Heath

                  under the trees last week,

        did I walk down the stairs?

Did I see love in a hut?

        With water and a crust that tastes like ashes

            (I am already ashes under your feet,

                  isn't that right?

            And when I saw crusts in your hands

did I believe you were actually eating them?

The question is: do you drink water

                because you like it or because

                    you live in a hut?

Did you see my better self recoil

      on the hill alone without love at my feet

            with love walking away from me

            and in step with some other figure?

        And who recoiled their feet at this figure

        when you walked in step without me

and never looked back?

And was it even you? On Hampstead Heath?

                  Last week?

The calendar of a dying man (part 3)

DAYS DAYS DAYS

The wait of a life drips from me

on the ground, soaked up

      I   can't   draw   it

      out   again.

I am an average man – average number of words per line – is
my ratio off?

I only have days to correct it.

What are my concerns?

The sting of a leg-hold trap that

can't be salved. Love that never dies

or divorces, haunting me as I lay here, the ceiling jumping.

Could I

cough you out

of my body like a bad spirit,

could you

remove death?

DNR?

You can't bring me back from the ground this time, love. You can only blow a kiss to death.

I am allergic to those black clothes.

> *And please, don't cut your hair.*

My brother had the same fate. Was scarred double

on my throwaway heart.

> (Did you feel the scar when you
> tongued on the inside?

The exam is over.

> Separation

> is final.

> Put your pens down and count back from ten.

> Any last

> words?

My dear Fanny,

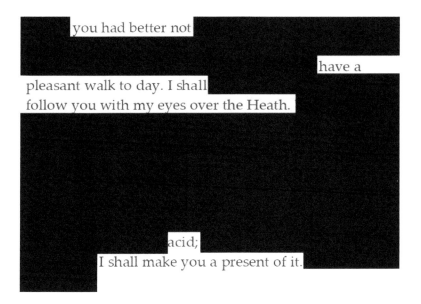

you had better not

have a
pleasant walk to day. I shall
follow you with my eyes over the Heath.

acid;
I shall make you a present of it.

J. Keats

PS.

I have no excuse   no excuse.
Forgive me

I am in deep love

you take possession of me

manifested

at the first sight

In case of the worst

what hatred shall

I have for another!

The calendar of a dying man (part 4)

HOURS HOURS HOURS

The heart beats

4,800 times. Eleven earthquakes move tectonic plates and we can never

go back, Fanny. The map is redacted

the map lies

to the left brain my brain will be left

to poetry,

not science.

How can a

drowning man

not hate

the way waves

continue to thrash?

The interrogation

Is a thing of beauty a joy for ever?

It will blind you with tears (Loving you is hard).

Does its loveliness increase?

I am trying to be truthful (I'm sorry).

Will it never pass into nothingness?

Its fierce kiss will stay on your lips (I will always love you).

Are we wreathing a flowery band to bind us to the earth?

It is a moon wrapped in brown paper (I read that somewhere).

Was it made for our searching?

Lethal (The acid thing was a bit much tbh).

Do we merely feel these essences for one short hour?

Its platinum loops shrink to a wedding ring if you like (But we're
so young).

Is each pleasant scene growing fresh before me?

Its scent will cling to your fingers, cling to your knife (I feel like
we're bad for one another sometimes).

P.S: John, I think we need to talk. Fanny

I gave you my heart though?

The beating is not love, it is the sound of the four valves
of the heart closing, opening, closing.

ARE YOU OPEN?

Heart cells don't divide – I won't divide and conkers are
spiky in their shell – but you, Y-O-U are… smooth like
mosaic tiles.

CAN I DECONSTRUCT YOU?

My left atrium is three times thicker than my right.

ARE YOUR WALLS TOO THICK TO PENETRATE?

45 seconds is all it takes to feed my body with my heart.
45 seconds of turning me inside out at least once a
minute.

SPIN THE BLOOD. MAKE IT NEW.

Your atrium is not an entrance hall.

THERE ARE NO CHAIRS.

My already failing left lung is narrower. Give me 'right
love' to keep me in business, Fanny.

YOU KNOW, A HEART CAN BEAT OUTSIDE THE
BODY BUT CAN I GIVE IT AWAY?

The corneas receive none of the blood that pulses for
you.

HOW CAN IT BE – (MY HEART SAW
YOU FIRST)?

The greatest threat is disease of the heart. Is the core
rotting, migrating across my chest, into the pockets of
moments with you...

DO YOU LOVE ME NOW MY INSIDES ARE THICK
WITH TARRED, BLOODIED MOULD?

Your ventricle is a little belly.

DOES IT HUNGER FOR ME?

Have some dark chocolate, my dear, and forget about
hearts broken up into sections.

CAN YOU LABEL THIS HEART WITH NUTRITIONAL
INFORMATION? ARE YOU
BAD FOR ME IN PART
OR BAD FOR ME

COMPLETELY?

How not to fall in love

To John

Love Frank (your *Romantics Anonymous* buddy)

1) Don't slide into her DMs unless she slides into yours first.
2) Don't like all 1283 of her photos retrospectively.
3) Don't comment on all of her 1283 photos, especially if she's with 'some guy'.
4) Don't get blinding drunk and get the night bus to her place.
5) Don't try to climb up the drain pipe and fall on your arse.
6) Don't write one hundred and seven poems about her.
7) Definitely don't share them on every social media channel you have.
8) Don't text her ag-
9) Oh, never mind.
10) Put the phone down.
11) Be nice to her friends.
12) Not too nice though or they'll think you're trying too hard.
13) Not everyone cares if you're a poor poet, they might just like you for being you.
14) Don't smoke thirty cigarettes in a row and feel sick for days.
15) Don't write one hundred and *eight* poems about her.
16) Try to remember who you were before you met her.

17) Spend some time with your friends.
18) Join *Romantics Anonymous* if that doesn't work.
19) Follow the steps. ~~Not hers.~~
20) Don't tag her again. PLEASE JUST STOP.
21) Don't steal pens from waiting rooms to write about her using different inks (???).
22) Write it down. Write it down.
23) NOTE: <u>Burn at least fifty percent of it.</u>
24) Remember that her feet are not only tolerable but beautiful.
25) Know when to let her come to you.
26) Don't overwrite her beauty. Just love it.
27) Stop throwing stones at her window. (*It's so last century...*)
28) Don't forget TB might be curable but being a twat of a boyfriend is terminal.
29) Write about trees.
30) ...Please don't fall in love with a tree. Just saying.

The calendar of a dying man (part 5)

MINUTES MINUTES MINUTES

love is my religion love is my religion love is my religion love
is my religion love is my religion
love is my religion love is my religion love is my religion love
is my religion love is my religion
love is my religion love is my religion love is my religion love
is my religion love is my religion
love is my religion love is my religion love is my religion love
is my religion love is my religion
love is my religion love is my religion love is my religion love
is my religion love is my religion
love is my religion love is my religion love is my religion love
is my religion love is my religion
love is my religion love is my religion love is my religion love
is my religion love is my religion
love is my religion love is my religion love is my religion love
is my religion love is my religion
love is my religion love is my religion love is my religion love
is my religion love is my religion
love is my religion love is my religion love is my religion love
is my religion love is my religion
love is my religion love is my religion love is my religion love
is my religion love is my religion

    but what is love?

The calendar of a dying man (part 6)

SECONDS SECONDS SECONDS

A

~~look~~ lock of your

-hair is a chain across

oceans. The rust

-the blood. Copper in

case encasing

-me in a tomb. I am rapt

-in layers of you –

-on both sides. You

-are my volta   -in real-time,

-turning

-me ~~awry~~ away

from the night but

-the tunnel…

What   light is

~~there~~

                                                    at the

                                                    end of

                                                    a cavern

~~off~~ of

                        dirty blood?

To… something else

Decondition of   clearness and /// **jarring** ///

barrenness.

Conspiring with her how to damn
the space around (   ) dead leaves (   ),
to straighten with bananas
those plain house bulbs
& **empty** all fruit of immaturity.

To shrink the shell, and slim
the interior [without a dark edge],
and a more unready adult
and still less…

Younger
trees
for the
insects

until they suspect cold _____ will always per cyst
for autumn has voided their warm-hearted **caverns**.

WHO HAS RARELY CAUGHT
ME OUT OF YOUR DEBT?
Whoever doesn't look may not always lose.

You   standing alert —
your skin pressed down by the pre-selected rain.
OR, on a fully-wasted   straight line
wide awake.
Vigilant with the absence of poppies, while you
squander the final vast space.

But, none of these untwisted branches
And often, you do not remain wobbly
with your unburdened feet / _{across a ditch} /
Or away from a cyder-press, an impatient scowl.

You ignore the closings - minute - bye - minute.

Where are the **silences** of autumn?
NO, WHERE ARE THEY?
Don't think about them, you have
your silence, also.

Meanwhile allowable clouds
decay the hard-living week.
And avoid the barren sky.

Then in a joyous ensemble the giant beings
celebrate *separate from the land stones,
miscarried below*,
or floating as the dark rain breaks or breathes.

And so, newly born humans quietly whisper from flat
methods.
Portal injuries cry, and later, with throaty lightness!
The blue backbone hisses
from an open landscape
and dispersing creatures
sob in **limbo**.

The calendar of a dying man (part 7)

MOMENTS

your final token suffocates and releases

physicality is the only bridge – to touch to live

too loved?

EQUATION:

SUPERIOR VENA CAVA

oxy-starved love

INFERIOR VENA CAVA

…distract me forever

Fanny.

My dearest Girl,

to be separated
from you
or whether it will not be worse than your
presence now and then,
think of it as
little as possible.

You know our situation –
what hope is there

read poetry   write it.
I cannot say forget me –
impossibilities
not strong enough to
be weaned –
Happen what may

J-K-

Having dull opiates with you (too late)

After Frank O'Hara

Being in love with you was even more fun than
dull opiates and walks on Hampstead Heath and the
nightingale's song
partly because of your intolerable feet
partly because those feet were not intolerable when they
walked with me
partly because of your love for poor poets
partly because your mum hated me
partly because you wrote me goodnight notes that I would
later burn and no one will know your side of the story now
but you will keep my letters as if I were important to you in
between the trees when we walked never quite touching never
consummating whatever this was I stared at you
and I would rather have stared at you than the autumnal
landscape from atop a hill while wandering through lifeless
trees not thinking about my death except
when I remembered you would marry someone else and then
I thought about Chapman's Homer and the shore
and thank goodness I could show you these things before
you had to wear black all the time and people judged you
for your intolerable feet in those intolerable shoes just as I did
at first but now I know your feet are beautiful it's just
I didn't think properly at first and now I lament that I wasted
the little time we had thinking of your faults and maybe
re-reading Chapman's Homer I didn't see the faults there too
and I should've seen mine and this is why I am telling you
about this

Love me for ever-

Gavel grave on our chests.

> *Breathe in. Breathe out.*

Judge now, Fanny.

You overrated me, like giving 5 stars to

Ferris Bueller's Day Off.

(I know some people love it

but seriously, he's a douche.)

I CONFESS: words were beautiful and barbed, hiding razors

under the tongue.

A convict convinced – always looking for the tunnel

away from polluted blood.

Did we escape the crushing impact

of our rib cages? Did we escape the slow

> *Breathe out. Breathe.*

deflation of love?

Did you give your heart to a rung-ed man, never able to climb, to put my head over the parapet?

The head already splintered – fragments of

you tú you tú you tú you

words & consonants & vowels & vows to love

forever but

misspell… four ever?

But Fanny, love was your tolerable feet my
intolerable scars.

The doctor drained lifeblood,

transfused you out,

but in moments   (the last moments) –

lungs flooded with breathless desperation.

Breathe for us both.

*Where were
you at*

that minute,

the second?

You were 5 out of 5, bright star. A constant beat, never missing

my heart. Now terrible, quiet heart.

No beating

under

the
floorboards.

No.

Where did breath go?

Your words: "Good night"

under my pillow. Where I lay my head,

you
lay ahead
(without me.

**Remember me to the
world / wear a duffle coat.

The
words cold without

you, icicles

under my

eyelids, for eyes

never open.

I died easy / loved hard.

With no lungs, no lungs

to suck

you inside.

QUESTION: who killed whom?

My name was water was ice was flooded was a sea.

Did we see past the selfie, the filter, the profile, the surface –

the grease of butter?

FANNY, HERE LIES ONE

WITHOUT TWO.

wish to forget you?

stretch my mind

to forget you for your

own sake

to part from you.

doors and

windows.

send me my goodnight. Remember

J-K

WAKE UP

Thought there would be light but there's…

HEADLINE NEWS: FANNY BRAWNE

in a relationship with Peter Tyler

Beep beep beep beep beep

beep beep beep beep beep

beep beep beep beep beep

beep beep

My stinging lungs, carving with each intake. P3t@r. T]l@r. What does that mean?

The valves of my heart opening and closing

[the openings are trap doors].

F

      A L   L

 I   N   G

THROUGH – GAPES

Here,

swallow this.

GULP GULP GULP.

Who is a ghost – the nurse or Fanny?

A total of 1.5 million people died from TB

(in 2018)

Not me.

The end was no stop, the end was an ellipse.

MISSING: 5 months of my life?

Have I time travelled to Hell?

An estimated 10 million people fell ill with tuberculosis (TB) worldwide (in 2018)

How do you spell ac-he. My stomach is a cavern where love visited but now love has wandered away from the group / I could eat (((((((((((((the world and still be hungry.

Urgh, Fanny, Peter uses hashtags like blinking. It's all: *#livingmybestlife #perfectgirl #yolo #bestdayever #breakfastinbed*

Did you even like my poems?

TB is curable and preventable

Let's go back and pre-vent me before I reached you. I'll drop right down into the floor before we met, before I saw your good/bad mouth.

Is love preventable? Has our love cured like meat and isn't that how it's meant to be?

> *I keep*
>
> *swallowing*
>
> *these*
>
> *pills.*

An estimated 58 million lives were saved through TB diagnosis and treatment between 2000 and 2018

Note for later: check the definition of 'saved'.

Ending the TB epidemic by 2030 is among the health targets of the Sustainable Development Goals

NEW LIFE GOALS

- Lose the five-month beard
- Overcome the heartbreak
- Visit some new countries
- Embrace living life again

Shit,
I've done it
again.

Okay, erase ~~LOVE~~

Negative capability is
a blank page

Hannah

07982 333 568

You're not my patient anymore. Call me?

***

EXPLANATIONS

How we met: Writing a paragraph, closing the document, rewriting from memory and adding some of my own words, as well as quotes from Keat's letter about his first meeting with Fanny

Love ambition and poetry: Using Oulipo + N7 method approx 7-10 places above or below the featured words in the dictionary

I know not where to go: Includes some found material from:

John Keats – The Eve of St Agnes, E. E. Cummings - i carry your heart with me (i carry it in my heart), William Shakespeare – Sonnet 18, Elizabeth Barrett Browning – How do I love thee?

Call me: Written on my skin, photographed and cut up using Paint, then words added on top.

To Fanny: A partly-synonym, part-invention interpretation of the sonnet 'To Fanny'

next to of course: Using found material from E. E. Cumming's poem 'next to of course god america i', 'On First Looking into Chapman's Homer' by John Keats, and extracts from his letters to Fanny Brawne

Fanny if by any other name: Sources: classicthesaurus.com, nameberry.com, synonyms.com

Throw me to the wind: Redaction of 'Ode on a Grecian Urn'

Annotations on a poet: Found material from my school study notes on Keat's poems

I have fears when: Response to 'When I have fears I may cease to be'

Des humains san amour: A rewriting of 'La Belle Dame Sans Merci' combined with found material from 'The End of the Affair' by Graham Greene

The Interrogation: A combination of extracts from 'Endymion' and 'Valentine' by Carol Ann Duffy

To… Something: Antithetical translation of 'To Autumn'

Having dull opiates with you (too late) A rewriting of Frank O'Hara's poem 'Having a coke with you'

Blackout letters (various) Using Keat's original letters to Fanny Brawne, I created new blackout poems

Thanks to these publications for featuring some of these poems: Full House Literary Magazine, Adjacent Pineapple, Selcouth Station, Beir Bua Journal, Howling Press magazine, The Abandoned Playground, Untitled Writing Voices, Poem Atlas.

Thanks to those who gave me feedback and supported this collection, especially Lydia Unsworth, Ollie Charles, Leia Butler, Trini Decombe, Alec Newman, Sarah Gibbons, Katy Wareham Morris, Rachael Charlotte and anyone I have forgotten because I'm not perfect!

About the author

Nikki Dudley is managing editor of streetcake magazine and also runs the streetcake writing prize and MumWrite. She has a chapbook and collection with KFS. She also has a pamphlet with Beir Bua. She is the winner of the Virginia Prize 2020 and her second novel, Volta was published in May 2021.

Website: www.NikkiDudleyWriter.com **Twitter**: @NikkiDudley20

Facebook: NikkiSDudleyAuthor **Insta**: @nikkisdudley

Praise for the Author

"In the tradition of Leonid Tsypkin's *Summer in Baden Baden* and Ali Smith's *How to Be Both*, Dudley playfully reimagines a historical passion; here twisting and dragging the collection's source material through the bulging intestines of modern-day self-making, resulting in a heady cacophony of post-post-classical internetism. "How do I love thee? Let me fragment the ways."

- **Lydia Unsworth; poet, latest collection out with Beir Bua Press**, *Some Murmur.*

"Such a thrilling time to be a reader; this collection takes us ziplining across new terrain, a dead poet, his lover, the male gaze, old fashioned love repurposed for modern times. The original words of love filtered through apps, texts, the internet and Dudley's unbounded imagination. There is real love here, but not between the main players but from Dudley and her love of the written word and Keats, it is palpable and resonates these experiments to bowed head at prayer time."

- **Michelle Moloney King; poet, visual poet, editor Beir Bua Press.**

"Fanny B. Mine is visually, structurally, and linguistically brilliant. I loved every letter of this collection, Nikki has created something truly amazing. At times humorous, and always thought-provoking, Fanny B. Mine is an intriguing exploration into the relationship between Keats and Fanny with a modern twist."

- **Leia Butler; writer and head editor of Full House Literary Magazine.**